Cornish Place Rhymes

A.L. ROWSE
(1903-1997)

A COMMEMORATIVE VOLUME

CORNWALL BOOKS

First Published in 1997 by Cornwall Books

CIP Catalogue Record for this book
is available from the British Library

ISBN 1 874448 32 9

CORNWALL BOOKS
is an imprint of Halsgrove Publishing

HALSGROVE
PUBLISHING, MEDIA AND DISTRIBUTION
Halsgrove House
Lower Moor Way
Tiverton, Devon EX16 6SS
Tel: 01884 243242
Fax: 01884 243325

Printed and bound in Great Britain
by Bookcraft Ltd, Midsomer Norton

Preface

Cornwall's greatest literary son, historian of international renown, man of letters, and poet, A.L. Rowse, died on 4 October 1997 at the age of 93.

Born at St Austell in 1903, his roots among the clay-workers of Tregonissey, he entered Oxford University, excelled in his studies, and later became a Fellow of All Souls - an event he described as being the most important of his life. His subsequent classic books on the world of Elizabethan England, and his study of Shakespeare's sonnets are the works by which his international reputation was won, but his Cornish books will remain the most enduring - certainly in the hearts of his fellow countrymen.

I grew up not a stone's throw from the village of Trenarren, which A.L. Rowse chose to make his home. His reputation went before him and, as boys, we passed the impressive gates of Trenarren on our way to the beach, hoping to catch a glimpse of the Great Man in the sunlit gardens. The truth is that he was seldom there in those days, although he once addressed the assembled pupils of my school in St Austell. He spoke to us about the importance of historical study in much the way he proclaimed to his students at Oxford, supremely confident in his own academic expertise. He talked at great speed oblivious of the fact that most of those whom he addressed were left floundering far in his wake.

In later years we corresponded occasionally on matters related to publishing books about Cornwall. He know the value of his reputation in bookselling terms and was never slow to suggest that if I was not agreeable to publish a work he would easily find someone who was - which he did! I have only one regret in this, that, when asked, I did not republish his superb book, *The Cornish in America* - although it did not remain long out of print.

In 1996 the Great Man and I met again through James Mildren, newspaperman and writer, who persuaded his friend to record some of his Cornish verse and reminiscences. The resultant audio tape, *My Cat and I Grow Old Together*, recorded with A.L. Rowse sitting up in his bed, is a wonderful reminder of the man's truly extraordinary mind and his boundless enthusiasm, even at the age of 91. James himself was a fund of wonderful stories of 'Lesley' and we conspired to get more of the Great Man's memories down on tape. Sadly, A.L. Rowse suffered a stroke a month or so after our first recording and tragically James died in January 1997 and our plans came to nothing.

At the time of the recording Dr Rowse asked me to publish this book of rhymes and I asked James to provide a foreword. On James' death the project lost momentum. In one of the last letters I received from the author he made it clear that this little book was a favourite of his Cornish writings and one that he was most anxious to see in print. In the same letter he described his excitement on hearing that one of his books had been included in the sale of the late President John F. Kennedy's library, a signed copy. "Where it came from I've no idea, I certainly didn't give it to him...".

It is fitting that this posthumous work, his last, should be about his beloved Cornwall. It is dedicated to his memory and to his friend James Mildren.

Simon Butler
Halsgrove 1997

Contents

INTRODUCTION

When Dr Johnson was sleepless at night he occupied his mind composing Latin verses. Similarly when I can't get to sleep I take to making rhymes on Cornish place names. They take the form of couplets, regular or irregular; though I am amused to note that alliteration often comes spontaneously to aid.

Many up-country people find our place names fascinating, some difficult, others merely comic, for example, St Jidgey or St Ingunger, Praze-an-Beeble or Rose-an-crowse. This little collection will help them with pronunciation. For instance, Fowey is properly pronounced Foy - as it was spelt in earlier centuries; and it would be sensible to revert to it.

At Oxford I have noticed people with a classical background liable to start with Mega, for Meva, in Mevagissey. Note also that those ss's are pronounced as zz's.

For Cornish folk, at home, this booklet should find several uses. In schools it should help pupils with the geography of their native county. I remember that, long ago, my schooldays were completely wanting in that respect - it has taken me a lifetime to catch up. Here is a short-cut, at any rate a help.

The great majority of our place names are in the old Celtic language, as in Wales or Brittany. Many people will know that:

By Tre, Pol, or Pen
Ye may know most Cornishmen.

A thousand of our place names begin with Tre; after that prefix, m mutates to v, in the distracting Celtic way. So our place names offer an introduction to the language - as much as it is useful to know. At least it is frustrating not to know what the places mean or signify; one wants to know, and often they have become so rubbed down, rubbing shoulders with English over the centuries, that some have become difficult. We do not need to become Place Name experts, but we like to know what we can.

Most of our names are topographically descriptive. Truro, for instance, gives us the meaning of the three roads that determined its location. Many names will give us some indication of the history of the place. Penzance, the holy headland, points to the medieval chapel that stood on the headland there, represented now by St Mary's parish church. Bodmin - the second syllable points to the monks of St Petroc, whose monastery dominated the town up to the Reformation. Padstow is a shortening for Petroc's-stow, where his monastery originally stood, until removed inland for more safety from deplorable Vikings and other vandals.

We are already reminded that a whole section of Saints' names - I have not counted how many, from my native parish of St Austell onwards - refer to the numerous missionaries who came to evangelise our people - like John Wesley later - in the Age of the Saints, mainly the sixth and seventh centuries. Most of these came across the Bristol Channel - some of them went on to make a name in Brittany, like St Sampson who founded the diocese of Dol there, or St Mewan, who founded the monastery of St Méen.

A few of these Saints came from Ireland, St Ia, patron of St Ives, for example. Note that that name was earlier St Ies - the v is an English intrusion from St Ives in Huntingdonshire, nothing to do with us. In those Dark Ages travel by sea was easier than by land, obstructed by forests, marshes, and enemies. Turn a map on its side, and you will see that

Ireland, Wales, Cornwall, Brittany formed a western sea-world, with Cornwall at the junction of those sea-ways - for Tristram and Iseult, and King Mark to cross, as well as the missionary Saints.

A few names refer to function or folklore. Forms like hewas, as in Hewas Water, refer to the summer shieling when cattle were sent up to the moors and downs for pasture. In winter they were brought down to the lowlands, e.g. Gwavas.

And why should Trencreek be 'holy ground'? - Because it is on the site of a prehistoric barrow (crug for creek). Cornwall is encrusted with barrows, stone circles, menhirs (longstones), caers (round hill-forts), cliff castles, cromlechs (*cf* Grambla). Our place-names, however eroded or transmogrified, give indications of what is to be found or once existed there.

Altogether these Place Names give us a rich harvest to learn from or to play with. Those that are hardly explicable may serve their turn for Cornish Quizzes.

A.L.R.
Trenarren
St Austell

EAST CORNWALL

What sort of a joint
could one start at Torpoint?

One does not need to mince
Terms for beautiful Ince.

How happy to find a berth
In the old barton of Earth!

A single bachelor attorney
Lived a lonely life at St Erney.

The ancient family of Milliton
Did not reside at Pillaton.
On the village green at St Tudy
Expect to see Punch and Judy.

One has to be wide awake
To stay the pace at Landrake.

Should there be a gulf
Beside the bridge at Landulph?

It's not thought that Fitton
Painted at Lawhitton.

Lucky that the name Tregadillet
Rhymes with the law term 'quillet'.

The road junction at Doublebois
Doubles the traffic and the noise.

Try your legs and make a sprint
For the excellent pub at Pelynt.

Do you really pant
For a holiday at Lezant?

The old inhabitants of Bake
Never knew Siblyback Lake.

No one named Andrewartha
Lived in the house of Trebartha.

Do not yourself deceive -
St Ive is pronounced St Eve.

Parson Andrews made a merry
Old customer at Downderry.

The historic town of Liskeard
Should be held in high regard.

One could hardly grow an apple
At wind-swept St Ann's Chapel.

Going downhill at Gunnislake
Don't forget to apply the brake.

I'm rather at a loss
To recall Carminow Cross.

There was no place for a Megan
In the rectory at Warleggan.

It would hardly do to creep
Across the Devil's Leap.

If you wish to see Polapit
Tamar, Spring's best for a visit.

The old name of Tideford
Would have rhymed with Bideford.

At St Germans was a creek
Of the name of Cuddenbeak.

Is there any taker
For the tower of Maker?

A promising place for a filly
Is the fine park at Pentillie.

Try a game of tit-for-tat
On the top of Mount Ararat.

The Duchy castle of Trematon
Is not very far from Tamerton (Devon).

Nor is the parish of Pillaton
Many miles off from Rillaton.

Pare the sedges with a bill-hook
And take your boat around to Millbrook.

The historic family of Eliot
Had little footing in Menheniot.

The uncongenial place of Trelawne
Housed Trelawnys, of muscle and brawn.

The parish of St Pinnock
Is a far cry from Greenock.

The pronunciation of St Keyne
Rhymes, I rather think, with 'lean'.

I am charmed by Michaelstow,
A moorland parish you should know.

In the East perhaps St Dominick
May chime with Pencalenick?

One might have to steal
A lift to get to Carkeel.

Take a pen with a good nib
To record and write down Stibb.

It is not easy to put
A good rhyme to Herodsfoot.

Take your pony, put foot in stirrup
And make straightway to Tredarrup.

It might be hard to make a dash
In a country village like Trelash.

Whatever goes on at
A remote place called Splatt?

Eastern Treglasta
Answers Western Trewolsta.

Shakespeare's colleague Heming
Certainly knew not Botus Fleming.

The hamlet of Trelay
Has a neighbour in Tregray.

The queer name of Quethiock (Quethick)
Rhymes very well with Sheviock (Shevick)

Would you care to greet the dawn
Over the cove at Polhawn?

I consider quiet Milbrook
Might be just the place to write a book.

The Rouses - nothing to do with me -
Puritans, lived at Halton Quay.

From the hamlet of Cargreen
A view of the Tamar may be seen.

Would you care to push a barrow
Uphill to Harrow-barrow?

Eastern Collogget
Echoes Northern Pendogget.

I once knew fairly well
People who took name from Metherell.

Existence might be rather poor
On sequestered Kittow Moor.

The pleasant estate of Morval
Has an echo in Treworval.

The southern clan of Bodriggan
Owned no property at Fentriggan.

Can there by many
People at Lambrenny?

Pray, do not scoff
At the ghost of Trengoffe.

At Sheviock the wood of Perdredda
Gives us a clang for St Austell's Scredda.

Listen: you might hear a throstle
Singing in Tredrossel.

In the parish of Sheviock Blarrick
Provides rhyme for St Austell's Trevarrick.

St Germans' Tregonnock
Answers Mid-Cornwall's Boconnoc.

Eastern Polbathic
Echoes Western Bosvathic.

Would one be quite frantic
To occupy Lantic?

One would not care a piffle
For goings-on at Triffle.

The surroundings of Keverel
Would be right for a Metherell.

What goes on at Polsco?
I'm sure I don't know.

There is a curious story that
I have told of the Symondses of Hatt.

Would you care to find yourself moored
For good and all at Hessenford?

One might find it a gonner
To wager everything on Sconner.

Would one be able to keep awake
All day long at quiet Carslake?

The Kekewiches dug a trench
To make their house secure - Catch-french.

Could anything be well diviner
Than the lovely valley of the Lynher?

Away from the coast and cliff at Polhawn
And over the hill you find Liscawn.

I doubt if there is a single onion
Grown in the garden at Boconnion.

The gentlemanly family of Hill
Came into possession of Trethill.

On Bodmin Moor draw a bow at a venture
And you arrive soon at Bolventor.

The spectacle of Golitha Falls
Is one that for us never palls.

Hanbury-Tenison certainly fell
For what he created at Maidenwell.

How many houses, if you count,
Constitute the village of Mount?

On the Moor the tiny church of Temple
Is both complete and simple.

Those who live at Port-wrinkle
Know a mussel from a winkle.

The ancient hundred of Trigg
Was divided in two as much too big.

Stoke Climsland was Kelly-bray,
As it was known in an earlier day.

The quarries of Hantergantic
Look to the Moor, not the Atlantic.

The vanished mansions of Thanckes
Was well protected by its banks.

The farmplace of Penquite -
Is pleasant by day or night.

St Breward's farm of Penvorder
Echoes St Breock's Trevorder.

St Breward's farm of Carwether
Is not very far from St Clether.

Vestiges of Civil War cannon
Will hardly be found on the downs at Stannon.

It does not seem that any garret
Overlooks the bridge of Tresparret.

Unlikely that they use the harrow
On the high moorland stretch at Garrow.

From the main highway Trewardale
Looks very handsome in its vale.

The Domesday manor of Hamatethy
Chimes very well with Georgian Tredethy.

Blisand's historic Levethan
Salutes Gwennap's Trevethan.

May we couple Callington
With the Duchy's Tewington?

I doubt if one could catch a minnow
In the river at dear St Winnow.

Botus Fleming's Moditonham
Rhymes with English Puttenham.

The steep cliffs of Lantivet -
Contrast the gentle slope of Lanivet.

North Cornwall

Many an archaeological bone
Surfaced from the cliffs at Trevone.

One needs to be rather agile
To get across the gulf at Tintagel.

One would not know how to dispose
Oneself at exposed Trevose.

On the road to Perranzabuloe
You may meet any old so-and-so.

You could always publish banns
Of marriage in the church of St Agnes (pronounced Anne's)
Better wear your duffle
Coat at blowy Poughill.

If you wish to cheat the Devil
Try residing at St Eval.

'Pot, Kettle and Pan'
Rang the bells of Trevan.

Would one wish to make a cruise
Sheer from the cliff at Catacluse?

Festive St Endellion
Is a long way from St Mellion

Port Isaac is really Porth-issick,
Cove by cornfield - rhymes with physic.

A cosy place to nestle
Is the valley at Kestle.

Are the people of Bude
Much given to feud?

Was there an Anglo-Saxon slaughter
Ever at Canworthy Water?

The Camel looks rather wavy
From the front door at Pendavey.

Better keep your hat on
In the main street of Stratton.

Not much prospect of tin
In two parishes of Petherwin.

I doubt if Methodist Darite
Would allow one ever to get tight.

The famous quarry at Delabole
Makes a frightening great hole.

Life might be found harsh
Beside Crowdy Marsh.

Parson Hawker of Morwenstow,
An eccentric saint, had never a foe.

North-coast Bedruthan
Chimes with inland Truthan.

We wish all to enjoy
Long life at Treloy.

You might feel rather silly
At mistaking Rowtor for Brown Willy.

At Wadebridge do not fail
To visit the church of Egloshayle.

Our innocent Watergate
In Washington has a notorious mate.

Would it make a pleasant perch
To settle for good at Marhamchurch?

Retire from town and keep a dairy
At very rural Week St Mary.

The place is untidy 'like Launceston gaol'
So the old-fashioned folk would rail.

The good family of Petherick
Did not spring from Trebetherick.

The popular resort of Polzeath
Rhymes with south-coast Tywardreath.

Aesthetes arise! go forth
And improve Perranporth.

If you feel you're becoming a crock
Recruit your health and strength at Rock.

Do you pray or yearn
For the convent's peace at Lanherne?

The composer Granville Bantock
Was not a visitor to St Crantock.

What more perfect chancels
Than you see at lovely Launcells?

Admire the pure enamel
Of sunlight on the river Camel.

Is there a special order
Of ghosts in Tregagle's Trevorder?

The pronunciation of Launceston
Is very nearly that of Vanson.

It would need a rich fish-monger
Properly to equip Tresunger.

From the height of Wilsey Down
No sight of village, let alone town.

I doubt if the headland of Trevose
Is a proper place to doze.

The great tithes of Newlyn East
Were enough to provide an annual feast.

The tiny hamlet of Egloskerry -
Not large enough to make merry.

One does not expect to find pollack
In the trout streams of Trewollack.

John Wesley made no stint
Of preaching to the good at Trewint.

We wish them all joy
Who live at St Loy.

The historic hundred of Pydar
Had orchards productive of cider.

For Newquay St Columb minor
Sounds more chic and finer.

Padstow's Mayday Hobby-horse
Brings out the crowds in force.

The haunted vicarage of St Breock
Is much less gay than southern Feock.

I refrain from throwing a bouquet
To over-populated Newquay.

It can't be said the place is barren
Of books and papers at Trenarren.

On the long beach at Pendower
One could spend many an hour.

We may couple Heligan
With properly pronounced Bodrugan (i.e. Bodriggan)

I don't think scholarly Miss Batho
Was acquainted with Portscatho.

Who shall have dominion
Over Tregaminion?

Is perhaps Polkerris
Akin to Goonamaris?

Come and have a yarn
In the garden at Boscarne.

I did not know, to be frank,
Where ever was Higher Trerank.

Baptise an aunt
At St Sampson's Golant.

One needs a lot of strength to lassoe
A bull in a field at Penstrassoe.

Wouldn't it be somewhat cruel
To swim the long creek at Percuil?

Over the hill from Tywardreath
And across the Fowey you find Lanreath.

Loveday Hambly of Tregangeeves
Was rather good at raising beeves.

What is the story or romance
Of the ruined wing at Pennance?

The pretty drive into Pelyn
Dispels any thought of sin.

There is not very much room
For a mansion at St Stephen's Combe.

Daphne was not at all silly
To be so stuck on Menabilly.

Garibaldi's Englishman, of Penquite,
Was a stalwart man for a fight.

One would not wish to be tossed
Or gored by a bull at Costislost.

It is not a difficult search
To find the way to Winnard's Perch.

Do you feel a pressing hunger
To lunch or dine at St Ingunger?

What's o'clock
At St Petroc?

Was ever Rosteague
A place for intrigue?

One might encounter any day
A perfect downpour at Washaway.

The farm called Trinity
Speaks of infinity.

Many a man's muddle
Ended in Menacuddle (i.e. rocky well)

Many a man in youth
Was a miner at Polgooth.

Take a donkey and shay
And make straight for Pendrea.

The name of Luxulyan
Is pronounced like Tresillian.

I doubt if one would find it gay
To spend a lifetime at Bojea.

There would be a very few
Families at Menadue.

Would it be rather a dingy
Habitation at Melingey?

My old friend Howard Warrick
Lived a mile or so from Tregorrick.

The very name Nansladron
Points to sea robbers, a squadron.

Be careful of the approach
To climb the Rock at Roche.

See the cattle graze
On the downs at steep Carclaze.

One might easily come a cropper
At the cross-roads at Boscoppa.

The pure water of Phernyssick
Is quite as good as physic.

The endearing name Hallane
Makes for me a happy refrain.

The romantic ruin Restormel,
Round in shape, is not formal.

Is the farmland at Fentongollan
Specially promising for pollen?

Improbably the name of Trewoon
Rhymes precisely with Polruan.

Sequestered Ruan Lanihorne
Is not a place to scorn.

Up that steep hill into Tregony -
For coach and horses was agony.

The tiny hamlet of Polmassick
Is not the ground to rear a classic.

Is it possible the parish of Creed
Produces a credulous breed?

There is not enough
Folklore from Tremough.

Do not play fast and loose
With the chickens of Tregoose.

It was a pity when Grampound
Was a rotten borough found.

If we pronounce cabin - cabe-in
We then have a rhyme for St Mabyn.

Is there another mate
For neighbouring Lockingate?

One could never deplore
The charm of rugged Helman Tor.

Might one glimpse at Barn Park
The ghosts of former monks at dark?

Not much sign of mead or meadow
Among the clay burrows of Scredda.

The St Austell beach of Gwendra
Answers St Mewan's Hendra.

Enter the gate, follow the lane
Up to the grand garden of Trehane.

Good old Tresawna loved his dwellin'
Down the valley at Lamellyn.

One would not find a cannon
From the Civil War at Rosenannon.

Inland, echoes at Trethowel
Come from the coast at Carrickhowel.

Wesley was accustomed to dispose
Himself at welcoming Methrose.

You would not find a farrow
On the summit of Hensbarrow.

The road that runs through Stenalees
Will take you anywhere you please.

Beyond Roche you may rally
To the charming Ruthern valley.

The little parish of St Wenn
Grows plenty of pretty fat hen.

When young I knew well Tregrehan -
At Crinnis they used to cast the seine.

You may walk or ride or trundle
All the way up to Boscundle.

What odd nosy parker
Would want to live at Garker?

The little St Austell estate, Cuddra
Bears no relation to Treluddra.

Would you care to live at Trethurgy,
Or would you prefer to think of Rosemergy?

The village of St Stephen-in-Brannel
Lies midway between either Channel.

The inland parish, Treverbyn
Bears no relation to Port Quin.

The great engineer Trevithick
Was not aware of our Penwithick.

The rotten borough of Mitchell
Was not the home of Edith Sichel.

Walk in the park, enjoy the air
High up at expensive Penair.

At Christmas the monks sang *O radix
Jesse* at dear St Cadix.

Tregony's parish church, St Cuby
Does not quite rhyme with 'ruby'.

Our coastal cove Portholland
We take to answer Devon's Molland.

May we couple the mine at Bissoe
With the mining at Lambesso?

Could one gather a gallon
Of apples at Porth Avallon?

Driving along the road, 'Hullo!'
I say, 'here's Burngullow.'

Was there ever a deacon
At Belowda Beacon?

There's a chapel at Domellick,
And in Scilly a beach - Porthellick.

Several places are called Trenance -
Enough to swell a country dance.

May one couple the name of Bodmin
with unfamiliar Halwyn?

Scobell, an official of the Inns
Of Court, lived closed by at Menagwins.

If King Mark lived at Castle Dore
Remains a problem to explore.

Penventinue pronounces Pennytinny,
So linhay is pronounced as linney.

The Georgian house at Trewarthenick
Is not as pretty as Queen Anne Calenick.

My old schoolmaster H.I. Hugh
Was a farmer's bantling from St Ewe.

A bevy of Treffrys farmed at Rooke
For several generations, by the book.

In church and churchyard at St Kew
We find Treffrys, not a few.

The historic manor of Lantyne -
Would indeed that it were mine!

Sing the praises loud and louder
Of the ancient hundred of Powder.

At Fowey the mansion known as Place
To church tower turns a handsome face.

The inhabitants of Bodmin were near
Enough to poach salmon at Dunmere.

Years ago the ancient house of Penwarne
Was unappreciated, and forlorn.

Nothing under the counter
At rural Pellymounter.

It would not do to make a wager
On the Jacobites of St Columb Major.

Would one choose for an abode
The raw village of Grampound Road?

I doubt very much if Ladock
Is a place to buy a haddock.

Every year at Summercourt Fair
My poor old pa liked to be there.

No use being lazy
At industrious St Blazey.

One cannot hear the bells of St Mewan
Over the hill down at Pentewan.

Is the town of Mevagissey
To be preferred to Tregonissey?

One could create a pretty maze
In the upper field at fair Polglaze.

When passing by, do not speak:
This is holy ground: Trencreek.

The China-clay Trethosa
Must surely sport a girl called Rosa.

Blameless innocent Treviscoe
Today would have a beastly disco.

Enjoy a vacation at St Veep
Good Cornish cream and plenty of sleep.

WEST CORNWALL

There are several separate lives
To live and enjoy at St Ives.

Plenty of room to prance
On the quay at Penzance.

Reside at healthy Redruth
And enjoy a double dose of youth.

One would very soon be dead
If one fell from Vellan Head.

Unfamiliar Chyandour
Does that rhyme with sour?

One might naturally be afraid
To settle for good at lonely Grade.

No place is so remote and queer
As deserted Ardevora Veor.

We should pronounce Budock Vean (Vee-an)
Properly like Porthpean or Nanpean.

The artist's choice of Sancreed
Is a sacred spot indeed.

One might keep a tavern
At wayside Bosavern.

One need not feel much dudgeon
About rustic life at Ludgvan.

A summer stay at Porthleven -
The next step to heaven.

The sailing folk of St Keverne
Knew their way up the Severn.

Innocent St Anthony-in-Meneage
No place for amorous intrigue.

It somehow sticks in the gizzard
To think of the wrecks at the Lizard.

Low-church people would not swallow
Father Wason at Gunwalloe.

Bernard Walke was put in the pillory
For his proceedings at St Hilary.

At Queen Anne Killagorden
Lilian Knowles was heir and warden.

What sort of an imp
Would you place at Ventongimp?

An heiress might exhaust her
Fortune on Chysauster.

Do we care a doit
For Lanyon Quoit?

Take your place in Gwennap Pit:
Where Wesley stood you may sit.

Once-busy, populous St Day,
A ghost-town, no longer gay.

The skin of the parish of Mabe -
All granite - is not smooth as a babe.

One might develop quinsy
On the cliff top at Rinsey.

Do not try trepanning
At sequestered Halamanning.

We mostly reside far from
The bleak heights of Trencrom.

Have you the tools to fadge with
For building a boat at Cadgwith?

Is there anything to fear
From the ghosts of old Gwinear?

The Cornish Institute at Pool
Is where we need to go to school.

One would not appreciate a muggin'
Anywhere, even at Illogan.

I am not quite sure where is Troon
But perhaps I shall discover soon.

Of your charity, for St Just
In Penwith spare a crust!

The lighthouse of Godrevy
Is many a league from the Meavy.

In the garden at Trebilcock
I recall no sign of rock.

There are trees enough for a grove
In the vale at Lamorna Cove

I am one of the league
That much admires Tretheague.

The Spaniards paid a hostile call
Once, and burned the church at Paul.

Would one find a receipt for senna,
A potable medicine, at Boskenna?

There is no compelling cause
To prefer St Just to St Mawes.

The thought of planting up Tehidy
Is enough to make one quite giddy.

It would take me all day
To climb up Carn Brea.

For luck drop a pin
In the well at Penryn.

It is lucky that Madron
Gives a rhyme for Nansladron.

I should not like a python
To penetrate Bonython.

In all the long lane of Lanner
Do you think you'll find a tanner?

We should be sad, still sorrier
To miss the woods at Scorrier.

There must be a saintly myth
For the village of Mawnansmith.

The handsome garden of Penjerrick
Was made by a Fox, not a Meyrick.

Old Mrs Hext of spacious Treba
Was much superior to the name of Creba.

Bertrand Russell stayed at Treen -
Horridest humbug I have seen.

Virginia Woolf at Carbis Bay
Spent many a summer, many a day.

As elsewhere, the well at St Uny
Was used to convert the loony.

Noted for the birth
Of Davies Gilbert was St Erth.

The Tudor manor of Merthen
Was stone-built and not earthen.

The tanning family of Croggan
Were not natives of Illogan.

You might feel rather feeble
If knocked out at Praze-an-Beeble.

Is it possible you can't
Find house or home at Lelant?

Is the pleasant parish of Wendron
Specially good for the rhododendron?

I hardly think that the Eagle's Nest
Is a place propitious to rest.

Of sanctity a gushing fount
Was medieval St Michael's Mount.

The patron saint of Mullion
Was not in fact a scullion.

The ancient manor of Erisey
Couples well with Mevagissey.

The prolific clan of Luke
Might be lucky at Nancekuke.

A waste of waters - what a scene
From the promontory of Pendeen!

No possibility of ruth
In picnicking at Ponsanooth.

Sometimes you might note a goose
Beside the swannery at Burncoose.

How fine the headland of Penlee
Juts out into the encroaching sea!

The Queen Anne house of Trereife
Properly rhymes with reeve.

I doubt if you will find a tarn
On the summit of Tolcarne.

A wilderness of waves may be seen
From parts of the parish of Pendeen.

Is it so that St Buryan
Really rhymes with Veryan?

Two longstones stand at Drift
And an ancient cross one may not lift.

Crowse means cross, so Crowse-an-wra
Is a proper place to pray.

I do not think the tribe Trevenen
Originated from old Sennen.

What can be said of Constantine?
- More given to cider than to wine.

May we rhyme Cairn Olva
With neighbouring parish Morvah?

May we rhyme Pordenack
With remote Towednack?

What sort of a cargo
Would you choose for life at Spargo?

Tregonwell - or Tregonell?
Did that once rhyme with Tyrconnel?

Henderson's sister, I remember well
Ended up at Perranwell.

The cliff-side mine of Botallack
Answers the barton of Bonalleck.

Our estuary the Helford
Contrasts with Suffolk's Melford.

Behold the church of Old Kea -
Where the Saint came in from the sea.

We must make allowance
For the uglification of Clowance.

Do not guffaw or grizzle
At the good name Nanjisel.

The Quaker shrine Come-to-Good
Provides free spiritual food.

Treviades is pronounced Trevizzes -
A useful tip for Cornish quizzes.

St Martin-in-Meneage sports Mudgeon:
How far is that away from Ludgvan?

Should one pronounce the name Breage
To rhyme with 'league', or older' vague'?

In westerly Treworgan
We have an echo for St Mawgan.

We find we are not willing
To tramp the trackway to Goongilling.

What find is there that's any good
Hidden away in Grambia Wood?

I am rather at a loss
To know where's Nanjarrow Cross.

Couple together Landewednack
With still more remote Towednack.

We are rather surprised to know
The name Trebarva Goodinow.

The westerly place Trengilly
Is still not neighbourly to Philleigh.

Are we free to roam and rove
Around the places called Trengove?

The remote place Rose-an-crouse
Is not a residence for a Rowse.

It might be good to inherit Rosewarne
The leading house in all Camborne.

Mrs Delany lived at Roscrow
When Mrs Pendarvis, as we well know.

What is there that is dingey
About Goonhingey?

There was sometimes a rumpus
At Gwennap's Goongumpus.

Gwennap's manor of Cosawes
Signals to the castle of St Mawes.

Several places are named Gear
Besides that at Gwinear.

Would you prefer to leap
Or creep all the way to Pengreep?

Take a pleasant ramble
To the farm at Tresamble.

One regularly heard a bang
From the mine at old Ting Tang.

Perhaps it's as well to waddle
All the way to Trehaddle.

When mining prospered it was nice
To own some shares in Poldice.

The handsome hamlet, Perranarworthal,
Answers well to western Treworthal.

The Furry dance makes merrier
The ancient Hundred of Kerrier.

Gwennap's manor of Pensignance
Had much early significance.

An archdeacon built Porthgwidden
Upon an old historic midden.

One wouldn't wish to be caught in a blizzard
Sailing off the reefs of the Lizard.

Follow the highway without a bend
And straight you'll come then to Land's End.